When, in the summer of 1969, Astronauts Armstrong and Aldrin took man's first step on a heavenly body beyond our own planet, they marked both the end of one decade of space conquest and the beginning of another. What happens next as we continue to push back the frontiers of space and go on to explore not only the Moon but other planets in our solar system as well, is the subject of this absorbing and fascinating book. The author gives a detailed account of the next planned Apollo flights and their probable landing sites on the great rilles and craters of the Moon; the experiments future astronauts will perform there and what is expected to come from them; what scientists hope to learn from the Moon rocks brought back to Earth by Apollo 11; the surface rovers and jet-powered vehicles presently being built for use not only on the Moon but perhaps one day on Mars. No longer "an impossible dream," Mr. Dwiggins describes the plans now being drawn for space shuttles, space station modules to be used as bases for manned explorations, and blue prints for building entire cities on the Moon! *Eagle Has Landed* is based on information gathered from the most authoritative sources and is profusely illustrated with dozens of exciting photographs and diagrams.

EAGLE HAS LANDED

EAGLE HAS LANDED

The Story of Lunar Exploration

By Don Dwiggins

Illustrated with Photographs and Diagrams

GOLDEN GATE JUNIOR BOOKS

SAN CARLOS, CALIFORNIA

This book is respectfully dedicated to the memory of Astronauts Virgil I. "Gus" Grissom, Edward H. White II, and Roger B. Chaffee, who gave their lives that others might one day set foot on the Moon.

SBNs: Trade 87464-140-3 Library 87464-141-1

CONTENTS

Cover: Nuclear Moonship proposal

FOREWORD

THE FIRST VISIT of a human being to a sister planet has been an exceedingly exciting event not only for the United States but for the whole world. This country has dedicated much energy and a good part of its technical abilities to the monumental achievement. This was done with the most complicated technology in the history of mankind and was not devoted to warfare but to the excitement of exploration, both technological and scientific. The science fiction which many of us read as boys and young men is now the real world. The only thing that remains from Buck Rogers is the use of the word "zap" (to describe small lunar craters). Many people have become so used to the fantasies of television that the excitement and fantastic nature of the real-life accomplishments do not seem to appeal to them. To most scientists throughout the world, however, the real excitement of the exploration of nature and space is the best excitement of all.

DR. GERALD J. WASSERBURG
Professor of Geology and Geophysics
California Institute of Technology
Member, Lunar Sample Analysis Planning Team
and a Principal Investigator
at the Lunar Receiving Laboratory

AUTHOR'S PREFACE

WHEN, IN THE summer of 1969, Astronauts Neil Armstrong and Buzz Aldrin took mankind's first steps on a heavenly body beyond his own planet, they marked both the end of one decade of space conquest and the beginning of another. The first trip to the Moon and back achieved the national commitment established in 1961 by the late President John F. Kennedy; it also marked the opening of a new era of scientific exploration of our nearest celestial neighbor, man's first stepping stone to distant planets of our solar system.

Within this new decade we shall see exciting new discoveries and technological achievements as we strive toward new national goals in space. The Moon will serve as our proving ground for daring projects which only yesterday were science-fiction dreams. A lunar orbiting space station housing up to one hundred men will serve as a base of operations for detailed exploration of the Moon, and as a prototype for a manned spaceship able to carry Earthmen to Mars and beyond. Still more wonderful are plans for building entire cities on the Moon itself.

On future Apollo flights and beyond, lunar explorers will extend their range of operations with strange-looking surface rovers and jet-powered flying vehicles, unlocking age-old secrets that will bring a new understanding of such things as the origin of the universe and of life itself. In this book the author hopes to take you along some of those avenues of lunar exploration, no longer impossible dreams.

DON DWIGGINS

ACKNOWLEDGEMENTS

RESEARCH FOR THIS book began ten years ago when the author, as Aviation Editor of the Los Angeles *Mirror*, began covering the mighty Apollo program. In the intervening years, as the dream of putting a man on the Moon became a reality, literally hundreds of scientists, astronauts, technicians and government employees were interviewed, to report the world's greatest technological achievement as it happened. To all of these persons the author is grateful for their individual help in compiling this volume.

Thanks also go to the following industry and government organizations for their invaluable help and guidance: Air Force Cambridge Research Laboratories; Bell Aerosystems Co.; Bendix Aerospace Systems Division; Boeing Aircraft Co.; California Institute of Technology; Department of Defense; General Dynamics Corp.; General Electric Co.; Grumman Aircraft Engineering Corp.; Hughes Aircraft Co.; Jet Propulsion Laboratory; Lick Observatory; Lockheed Aircraft Corp.; McDonnell Douglas Corp.; Martin Marietta Corp.; National Aeronautics and Space Administration; North American Rockwell Corp.; Northrop Corp.; TRW Systems, Inc.; University of California at Los Angeles and at San Diego.

EAGLE HAS LANDED

THE HISTORIC MOMENT came at lunar dawn, exactly 1:18 p.m. EDT, Earth time, a Sunday afternoon, July 20, 1969, a time when nearly a billion Earthmen and women watched and prayed for the safety of two American astronauts, about to touch down on the Moon.

The approach to landing had been a real thriller, the trickiest in the long flight experience of Apollo 11 Commander Neil A. Armstrong and his fellow explorer, Air Force Colonel Edwin E. "Buzz" Aldrin, Jr.

They called her Eagle, that ungainly, spidery spaceship in which Armstrong and Aldrin were shuttling to the lunar surface from the Apollo command ship Columbia, in which Lieutenant Colonel Michael Collins, USAF, orbited the moon 60 miles above.

For the first time, an Earthling was preparing to land on another world, culminating a dream of ages and opening the way to a whole new era of space exploration. There was no air to grip a wing and hold it steady, only the dancing, spitting tailfire of a licking rocket-plume.

Tense now, voices of the astronauts and the men of Mission Control, 240,000 miles away in a place called Houston, reassured each other with the landing litany.

"We got the Earth right out of our front window!"

"She's coming down beautifully!"

"Better than the simulator!"

"Velocity 1200 feet per second, altitude 21,000."

"Eagle, you are looking great!"

"Altitude, 4,000 feet. You are go for a landing."

"Rog, understand, we are go for a landing."

"Two thousand feet, we're go! Sit tight!"

"Four hundred feet . . . 300 feet . . . 200 . . . 100."

"Forty feet—we're picking up some dust."

"Thirty-five feet, we're drifting to the right a little."

(Commander Armstrong, from 450 feet altitude on down, was in manual control of Eagle, taking over from the automatic pilot, for immediately below yawned a gaping crater chock full of ugly rocks. Expertly he guided Eagle over the rock field to a clear area, swiftly, surely.)

Then—"Contact light! . . . Engine stop!"

There was a silence, a long moment, when people on Earth knew that at last mankind had been set free, free to roam the limitless reaches of deep space, to explore other worlds.

And finally, Armstrong again, his voice calm, proud.

"Houston, Tranquillity Base here . . . *Eagle has landed*!"

It was a strange new world, a virtually colorless world of weird rubble, silent as death, covered with a fine black powder.

"A magnificent desolation!" cried Aldrin.

To Armstrong, the Apollo 11 commander, went the honor of being first to set foot on another world, an event he described for those on earth to hear even as it happened:

"I'm at the foot of the ladder, the LM foot pads are only depressed in the surface about, uh, one or two inches, although the surface appears to be very very fine-grained as you get close to it . . . It's almost like a powder down there. It's very fine . . . I'm going to step off the LM now . . . *That's one small step for man, one giant leap for mankind!*"

It was more than that. It was the realization of a national goal, a 1961

Neil Armstrong maneuvered the LM to avoid crater.

challenge to American science and technology hurled by the imaginative and vital young President John F. Kennedy, to achieve a Moon landing and safe return in a single decade.

Armstrong, bending carefully to photograph the mark he had left, like that of a ski boot in powdered black snow, might well have thought of Longfellow's words:

> *Lives of great men all remind us,*
> *We can make our lives sublime,*
> *And, departing, leave behind us*
> *Footprints on the sands of time.*

Whatever significance that footprint held would be determined not by Armstrong, Aldrin and Collins, magnificent as their achievement was, but by the others who would follow, astronauts who would seek to fulfill mankind's new-found destiny in the ever-widening reaches of space.

The story of how the brave Apollo 11 crew went to the Moon and back already is a part of the American legend, a story that will be told and retold so long as the spirit of adventure moves men to seek new frontiers to conquer in the name of mankind. In the next chapter we will trace some of the beginnings of this incredible feat, for only by looking backward is it often possible to see what lies ahead.

Technologically, the first lunar landing stands as perhaps the greatest achievement of its kind in the history of civilization. Scientifically, however, Apollo 11 was only the beginning, the crude start in studying the vast environment in which planet Earth drifts as a lonely oasis in the hostile reaches of space.

At a time when a safe journey was more important than what new knowledge could be learned, weight limitations and time limitations imposed severe restrictions on what the astronauts could achieve during their brief stay on the lunar surface.

As it turned out, the decision to limit scientific equipment in favor of more fuel made the difference between success and a possible catastrophe—Eagle landed with all but a small percentage of its rocket fuel expended!

Back on Earth, scientists fretted while the first Moon men went through televised political ceremonies that used up invaluable time—their total time spent on their portable life-support systems ran less than 2 hours 48 minutes, at a cost of more than $10,000,000 a minute!

One hour 48 minutes after Commander Armstrong set foot on the lunar surface, he and Aldrin had completed deployment of the three scientific experiments brought along—a solar wind experiment, a laser

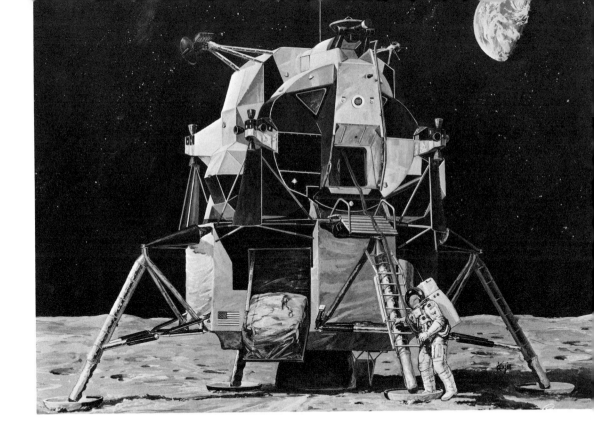

"That's one small step for man . . ."

experiment and a delicate seismometer. These experiments, the total weight of which was slightly more than 175 pounds, comprised the Early Apollo Scientific Experiments Package (EASEP).

As limited as these experiments were, they returned an almost immediate storehouse of data giving new clues to such perplexing mysteries as the origin of the universe. The solar wind experiment, left on the Moon for 1 hour 17 minutes, was a kind of window-shade device, sensitive to the bombardment of micrometeorites and particular radiation from the Sun. Alone of the three, it was returned to Earth.

Left behind on the lunar surface, the seismic device performed beautifully for the first lunar day, and soon after the Apollo 11 crew departed it transmitted to Earth what appeared to be a recording of a five-minute moonquake.

Also left behind, the laser ranging retro-reflector (LRRR) proved to be a frustrating and elusive device, as three Earth stations beamed at it tiny squirts of laser light, hoping to get back a reflection. These pulses, each only 100-millionth of a second in duration, chopped the laser beam into "pancakes" 2½ miles across and only 10 feet long. With this range finder scientists hope eventually to measure the Earth-Moon distance to within 1.5 meters. On August 1, astronomers at Lick Observatory in California first succeeded in bouncing laser beams off the LRRR, proving that it was effective.

Perhaps most stirring to the imagination was the collection of Moon dust and rocks brought back to Earth by Armstrong, Aldrin and Collins, geologic samples which afforded scientists of nations throughout the world the opportunity to begin a serious study of the lunar composition, in order to wrest from it more secrets of the Moon's nature and history.

One of the most controversial parts of Moon lore is the very nature of its myriad craters—were they formed by meteoric impact, by volcanic eruption, or both? Curiously, the first Moon rocks brought back by Apollo 11 only heightened the controversy. They appeared to be igneous, but were they formed as the result of an interior heating process, or by the searing temperature of a meteoric impact?

Many Earth scientists would be forced to change sides in the controversy, or at least reevaluate their thinking, on the basis of rock samples delivered to the Lunar Receiving Laboratory in Houston. One, Dr. Harold C. Urey of the University of California, a Principal Lunar Rock Investigator at Houston, admitted to a great feeling of humility on examining the Moon rocks.

Said Dr. Urey: "All of us who have been talking about the origin

Learning to walk on the Moon was a new experience for astronauts in one-sixth of Earth's gravity.

Setting up lunar surface experiments.

of the Moon should feel very humble ... nobody is right about it ... I think that no one had anticipated what we are finding, and I believe that no one has a good explanation of how it got that way ... The only thing we can do is wait for further data before we try to draw any good conclusions."

Tranquillity Base, where Apollo 11 landed, was number two of five original equatorial landing sites selected by the National Aeronautics and Space Administration (NASA) as compatible with mission requirements. It lay in the relatively smooth, shallow basin of a vast lunar "sea" (astronomers once thought these "seas" contained water and so named them *mares*)—the Mare Tranquillitatis, west of a prominent crater named for an eighteenth century British astronomer royal, Nevil Maskelyne. The Texas-trained astronauts gave other names to the lunar features in the vicinity of Tranquillity Base—Maskelyne W became the *Wash Basin*, and curious rilles, looking like dry gulches, were called *Diamondback Rille* and *Sidewinder Rille*, *Wagon Road* and *U.S. 1*.

The other four original Apollo landing sites stretched eastward across the lunar equator—Site 2 near where an unmanned spacecraft, Surveyor 5, had landed, also in Mare Tranquillitatis; Site 3 in Sinus Medii, where Surveyors 4 and 6 landed; Sites 4 and 5 in Oceanus Procellarum (Ocean of Storms), south of the prominent crater Kepler.

Actually, the selection of future Apollo landing sites may change from mission to mission, depending on what new discoveries each future flight accomplishes. In Chapter IV are listed the landing sites for Apollo 12 through 20 as projected after Apollo 11's successful visit to Tranquillity Base. To this list Dr. Urey would like to add visits to the center of one of the Moon's large circular mares, such as Imbrium or Serentatis. "Something filled up these smooth areas, and we ought to be finding out what's there," he commented.

Future mission planning calls for manned landings in the Moon's remote polar regions, and in fact anywhere on the surface that high interest dictates, such landings to be made possible by shuttling down from a polar-orbiting lunar space station. From these explorations, it is hoped, a more complete understanding of the Moon's physical

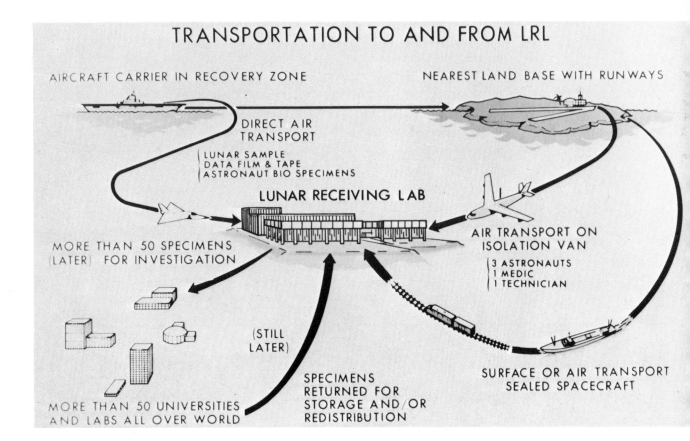

TRANSPORTATION TO AND FROM LRL

make-up will be possible than from the single rock collection from Tranquillity Base.

At Tranquillity, Armstrong and Aldrin scooped up samples of a fine black dust of over 50 percent glass. About one tenth of the dust sampling proved to be in the shape of very small beads and little dumbbells, the rest in the form of broken-up materials.

Said Dr. Urey upon examining the dust, "It looks as though the glass were made as the result of collisions. Very high temperatures appear to have been produced, for a moment, and rocky materials were melted and sprayed out or condensed from the gaseous stage, and fell on the surface of the Moon."

As for evidence of the existence of life on the Moon, "there is none whatever, there is very little of carbon compounds in the Moon samples," Dr. Urey said.

If Apollo 11's successful return of Moon samples raised more questions than it answered, scientifically speaking, it was still high adventure, not only for the astronauts themselves but for the world at large. Who did not thrill at Armstrong's beautiful landing, or at the televised image of Aldrin testing the now-famous "kangaroo hop" as a means of lunar locomotion? Under the Moon's light gravity, one-sixth that of the Earth, Aldrin found he could leap gracefully from 6 to 8 feet with each two-footed hop. And who did not smile when Aldrin acknowledged Eagle's clearance for takeoff for the long trip home: "Roger. Understand we're Number One on the runway!"

Thus, in the fall of 1969, the President's Space Task Group could foresee a thrilling future for manned lunar exploration in the years to come: "We believe that the new directions ... can be both exciting and rewarding for this Nation. The environment in which the space program is viewed is a vibrant, changing one ... Our planning for the future should recognize this rapidly changing nature of opportunities in space."

Astronaut Buzz Aldrin with American flag, stiffened with wires on windless Moon surface.

Going Home! Apollo 11 LM, the Eagle, approaches Command Module in lunar orbit, where Mike Collins snapped its picture with Earth in background.

THE FIRST CLOSE LOOKS

SINCE TIME IMMEMORIAL the Moon has been an object of man's curiosity, a dead, silent world of primordial rock, pocked by showers of meteorites, an incessant space rain of drifting debris of cosmic origin. To Earthmen long ago, the Moon had a peculiar beauty. They called it Selene, the Moon Goddess. The legend was told of her love for Endymion, a beautiful youth thrown into a deep sleep by Selene that he might be unconscious of her caresses.

More than 100 years ago, the great French novelist Jules Verne startled the world with a wild fiction story about three astronauts who traveled to the Moon and back inside a bullet-shaped aluminum projectile. Published as a novel in 1865, *De la Terre a la Lune (From the Earth to the Moon)* was amazingly prophetic of twentieth-century Apollo Moon missions which turned Verne's vision into reality in almost exact detail.

Verne went to the leading astronomers, aeronauts and other top scientists of his day and was thoroughly briefed on celestial mechanics and other physical laws on which to base his fantastic story.

His fictional astronauts — Captain Nicholl, Impet Barbicane and Michael Ardan—were launched from the mouth of a giant cannon Verne emplaced at the southern tip of Florida, not far from what is now Cape Kennedy. Just as Apollo 11 visited the Moon "for all mankind," so Verne had his spaceship financed by a world-wide public subscription.

Inside the projectile, Verne's make-believe space travelers carried a life support system of caustic potash and chlorate of potassium to replenish the air. Midway to the Moon they experienced weightlessness where Earth and lunar gravity were in equilibrium. Rounding the far side of the Moon, as did Apollo 10 in December, 1968, they gazed in awe at the startling lunar landscape from a low point in their elliptical orbit.

(Verne originated the modern terms *aposelene* and *periselene* to describe the highest and lowest points of the lunar orbit.)

His fictional spacemen observed winding dry riverbeds (we now call these *rilles*); marveled at the crater Clavius, which they decided was a giant volcano; were amazed by the crater Tycho, which Ardan described as the result of a comet impact. Crossing the southern limb in polar orbit, they studied two features that had long puzzled astronomers on Earth. One, the crater Newton, is so deep (29,000 feet) that the Sun never shines on its bottom. Verne's travelers likened it to "the mouth of hell." And on the glistening slopes of the Doerfel Mountains they thought they saw snow.

The book tells how, back at aposelene, Ardan applied a lighted match to the projectile's retrorocket, hoping to send it down to a Moon landing. Instead, so the story concludes, it sent the astronauts hurtling back to Earth, to splash down in the Pacific Ocean—not far from what was to be the Apollo landing site!

Scientific study of the Moon began in 1609, the year after a Dutch spectacle maker, Hans Lippershey, invented the telescope. Galileo Galilei in 1610 accurately described the Moon, as seen through a telescope, as a "world of mountains and chasms and contrasts of blinding light and total shadow." Johannes Kepler believed air and water existed on the Moon, as did Bishop John Wilkins who, in 1640, described dark spots on the Moon as water and predicted Earthmen would some day plant colonies there.

In this century giant new telescopes mapped the entire front surface of the Moon, yet it remained for rocketry to give man his first close look— by television. In 1964 and 1965 three Ranger spacecraft crash-landed on the Moon after returning 17,000 graphic views of potential Apollo landing sites. In 1966 the Russian spacecraft *Luna 9* and America's *Surveyor I* soft-landed to begin detailed close-up mapping.

From August 1966, through August 1967, five Lunar Orbiter spacecraft completed a detailed mapping of more than 99 percent of the Moon, front and back—a total of more than 14,000,000 square miles.

As a result of Orbiter and Surveyor photographs, NASA was able to select five possible Apollo landing sites from an original list of 30 along the lunar equator, within an area between 45 degrees East and West longitude and 5 degrees North and South of the equator. Orbiter completed this mission with three flights, leaving the next two for strictly scientific exploration. *Orbiter IV* was hurled into a polar orbit, and with a truly fantastic combination of spacecraft maneuvers and planning, mapped 99.5 percent of the Moon's front face in detail. *Orbiter V* was also placed into polar orbit so that photos taken from apolune (highest point in a lunar orbit)

1865 1970

1865 1970

1865

1975

1865

1970

would complete the backside coverage. Once the Orbiter missions were completed, they were sent crashing into the Moon to deaden their sing-song telemetry so it would not interfere with the coming manned Apollo flights.

During these unmanned flights we learned many new things about the Moon. *Ranger 9*, for example, scored a bull's-eye hit inside the crater Alphonsus, providing the first conclusive evidence of lunar volcanic activity. Alphonsus was chosen for a target because it was here, on November 3, 1958, that the Russian astronomer N. A. Kozyrev first saw a lunar eruption, of a gas containing carbon compounds.

This discovery renewed speculation that the Moon is still "alive" with a hot interior, like Earth's, and supported lunar theorists who believed many of the Moon's craters were caused by volcanic eruptions. They point significantly to the crater Aristarchus in the Ocean of Storms near the west limb, where, on the evening of October 29, 1963, a scientist at Lowell Observatory near Flagstaff, Arizona, was studying a curious feature called the Cobra Head in Schröter's Valley. At 6:50 p.m. the scientist, James A. Greenacre, a selenographer (one who studies lunar features) was startled to see two bright, ruby-red spots appear near Cobra Head. He called an assistant, Edward Barr. At 6:55 p.m. they saw a third bright spot appear inside Aristarchus and extend 11 miles along the rim. Greenacre said it was "like looking into a large polished gem ruby."

The phenomena was repeated a month later when a new red spot winked on Aristarchus' outer rim. Interestingly, both observations occurred when the lunar crust was under maximum stress, with the Moon in such position that Earth's gravity induced the strongest tidal action on its satellite.

This Earth-Moon-Sun alignment, called *syzygy*, exerts such a tidal influence on both Earth and Moon that we now feel there is a relationship between the formation of mountains on both bodies. Nikolai Kozyrev, the Russian scientist, writes: "Tectonic (rock formation) processes on the Earth and Moon are connected with each other as though the Moon were in direct contact with the Earth, that is, as if it were our seventh continent. This contact is established by endlessly moving time, and it is through this medium that the Earth, as the more massive body, maintains the Moon's power production and its cosmic life."

A good example of the awesome power of this tidal attraction at syzygy was the disastrous earthquake touched off in California's Kern County July 21, 1952. A CalTech geophysicist, Dr. C. Hewitt Dix, traced the quake to its epicenter on a fracture called the White Wolf Fault, which pointed almost directly at the Sun and a very new Moon, which together

Ranger spacecraft crashed into the Moon after taking first close-ups of lunar surface (right).

Lunar Orbiters returned amazing pictures of the Moon's frontside and backside (lower left).

Surveyors soft-landed on the Moon, returned detailed pictures and scientific data (lower right).

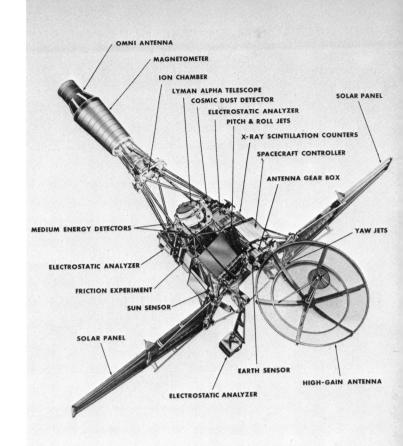

OMNI ANTENNA
MAGNETOMETER
ION CHAMBER
LYMAN ALPHA TELESCOPE
COSMIC DUST DETECTOR
ELECTROSTATIC ANALYZER
PITCH & ROLL JETS
X-RAY SCINTILLATION COUNTERS
SPACECRAFT CONTROLLER
ANTENNA GEAR BOX
SOLAR PANEL
YAW JETS
MEDIUM ENERGY DETECTORS
ELECTROSTATIC ANALYZER
FRICTION EXPERIMENT
SUN SENSOR
SOLAR PANEL
EARTH SENSOR
HIGH-GAIN ANTENNA
ELECTROSTATIC ANALYZER

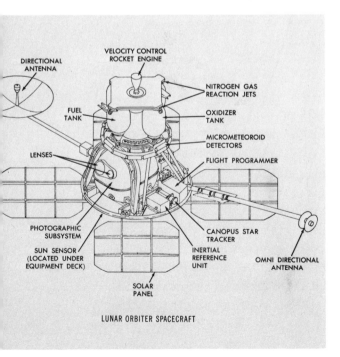

DIRECTIONAL ANTENNA
VELOCITY CONTROL ROCKET ENGINE
NITROGEN GAS REACTION JETS
FUEL TANK
OXIDIZER TANK
MICROMETEOROID DETECTORS
LENSES
FLIGHT PROGRAMMER
PHOTOGRAPHIC SUBSYSTEM
CANOPUS STAR TRACKER
SUN SENSOR (LOCATED UNDER EQUIPMENT DECK)
INERTIAL REFERENCE UNIT
OMNI DIRECTIONAL ANTENNA
SOLAR PANEL

LUNAR ORBITER SPACECRAFT

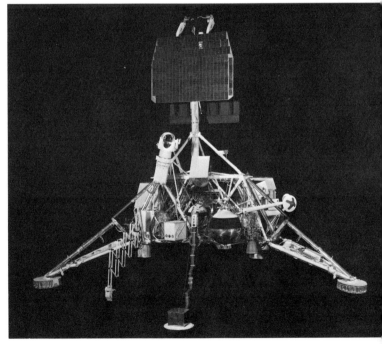

triggered the shock. The earthquake, worst in Southern California since 1857, cost 14 lives and caused $60,000,000 in property damage. Now scientists want to learn whether such disasters can be predicted through studies of moonquakes.

Other scientists believe that the Moon is a cold, dead body whose structure is unlike the Earth's molten interior and solid mantle, or crust. Dr. Harold Urey once gave the author another explanation of the so-called "degassing" observed on the Moon as being of meteoric rather than volcanic origin. Meteorites striking the Moon, he said, "probably contain carbides. Now, calcium or magnesium carbide, when treated with water, produce acetylene instantly. Acetylene is C_2H_2. As soon as this is exposed to sunlight the hydrogen would leave it, giving C_2, the gas observed by Kozyrev." The necessary water, he added, would "filter up through the surface, come in contact with calcium carbide, produce acetylene which would flow onto the surface of the Moon and produce the spectrum which Kozyrev observed."

To Dr. Urey's way of thinking, the gas observed coming from the crater Alphonsus was also probably C_2, coming from smaller inside craters formed by exploding acetylene gas. Most selenologists agree that the majority of Moon craters are meteor-impact craters, hence to learn more of the Moon's nature it is necessary to examine "raw" Moon rocks and not the rubble left scattered by eons of meteoric rain.

Of high interest is the crater Copernicus, the most prominent lunar feature visible from Earth, in the Sea of Storms. Believed formed by impact of a large asteroid, it also has clusters of smaller craters around its rim, which appear to be volcanic. Most intriguing are the walls and central peaks of Copernicus, which expose nearly four miles of vertical lunar crust, like the stratification seen in the Grand Canyon.

Then there is the mysterious crater Linnè in the Sea of Serenity, a feature which all but disappeared in a period of only 30 years. Where astronomer Bernhard Schmidt saw a crater 11 kilometers wide, astronomer Dinsmore Alter, three decades later, saw only a diffuse whitish area with no discernible crater at all. It has been suggested that Linnè is more like a hot spring than a volcano.

Examination of the Moon by telescope and unmanned spacecraft posed many exciting possibilities for future manned exploration, one of the most intriguing being the great collision site in Mare Imbrium, identified in 1893 by an astronomer, G. K. Gilbert, as the result of a catastrophic impact of some object 100 miles in diameter, which struck at less than the speed of sound. Whatever it was, it plowed up a vast area of the Moon and scat-

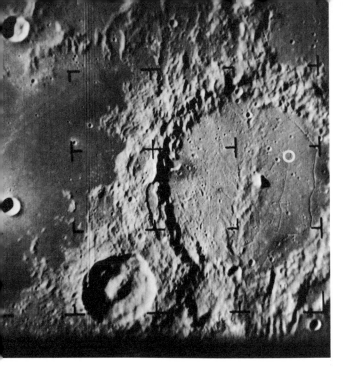

Remarkable sequence of pictures taken by Ranger IX prior to crash-landing in lunar crater Alphonsus. Small circle marks target as seen from altitudes of 265 miles, 95.5 miles, 12.2 miles and 4.5 miles. Alphonsus is the crater where Russian astronomer N. A. Kozyrev saw eruption of volcanic gas in 1958. Some believe this is evidence the Moon is "alive."

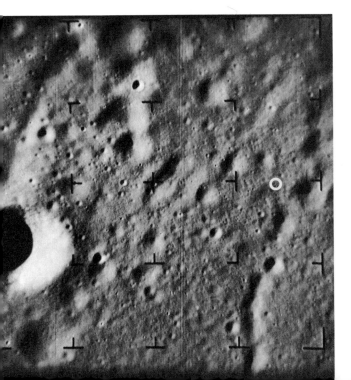

Surveyor V landed the first "chemistry set" on the Moon (upper left) to determine chemical composition of the Moon's soil by alpha particle scattering. At upper right, lunar rock fragment is remotely excavated by surface sampler on Surveyor VII. Below, a mosaic panorama of narrow-angle TV pictures shows trenches dug in the Moon's soil near crater Tycho. Large trench in center is 30 inches long, 9 inches deep.

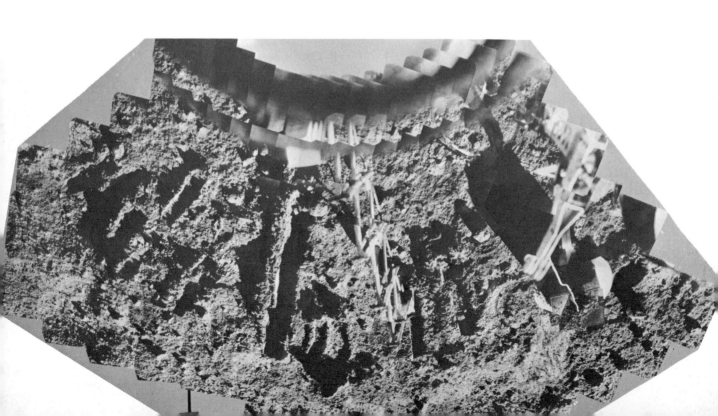

Surveyor VII shot these close-ups of lunar rocks and craters in highlands 18 miles north of Tycho. Horizon at center is 8 miles away. Below, Surveyor VII reveals the Tycho region as a forbidding area of boulders.

Orbiter I shot this breathtaking picture, historic first view of Earth from vicinity of the Moon. Below, Orbiter II took this remarkable picture of the crater Copernicus, looking north across the crater's southern rim. Mountains rise 1,000 feet from crater floor, while on the horizon a 2,000-foot mountain of the Carpathian Range can be seen.

Spectacular array of lunar domes appear in this Lunar Orbiter II photo to the southwest of Marius, crater at upper-right corner. Similar to Mt. Rainier and Mt. Shasta, and seen here for the first time in detail, they confirm that the Moon has had a long, complicated history of volcanic activity.

tered fragments of its own body, along with pieces of the Moon, for more than 2,000 kilometers across the central region of the Moon. Some of the débris fell on older craters and scarred the walls of others like Alphonsus and Ptolemaeus. Shattered and molten material settled into the present configuration of Mare Imbrium, leaving a number of faults, rubble piles and fields of granular and dusty materials.

Another lunar puzzle is the great crater Tsiolkovsky, on the Moon's far side, first photographed by the Russian *Lunik III* in 1959 and named in honor of Konstantin Eduardovich Tsiolkovsky, Russia's "father of rocketry." Photographed in sharp detail by Orbiters, Tsiolkovsky is revealed to be filled with an unusually dark substance.

The list could go on and on, of lunar points of interest revealed by telescopic and spaceship photography, as the men of Apollo begin to expand their fields of exploration—the mysterious rilles of the Harbinger Mountains near the crater Aristarchus, the extraordinary scarp of the Apennine Mountain front in the lunar highlands.

Here, in the highly cratered highlands, may be found quantities of upthrust "raw" Moon material—4.5 billion-year-old original solar system rock. Deciphering the story of lunar rocks is a complex task because of the widespread mixing and alteration of lunar rocks by meteoroid and asteroid fragments striking the surface—each impact of a meteor on the Moon throws out material with a mass estimated at 1,000 times that of the incoming projectile.

Thus, preliminary examination of the lunar rocks and dust returned to Earth by the Apollo 11 crew became the first step in the second phase of selenographic study, for now scientists have not only close-up photographs of the Moon, but actual pieces to examine. At best, these studies show more of the nature of the Moon in the Sea of Tranquillity area; a more complete understanding will come in bits and pieces as the exploration of the Moon continues in this and the next decade. (Some of the other Moon sites to be visited by on-going Apollo teams are listed in Chapter IV.)

Future scientific analysis of the Moon surface will be done with more and more sophisticated ALSEP (Advanced Lunar Scientific Experiments Package) equipment, as a follow-on to the early Surveyor missions. Those unmanned probes found that the chemical composition of the Moon's crust resembled Earth-type basaltic silicate in the mare areas; that the three most abundant elements in the mare areas are the same as those on Earth—oxygen, silicon and aluminum; and that molten magma from inside the Moon differentiated (formed different kinds of rocks), evidence that the Moon's interior was, and may still be, hot.

Dr. Albert R. Hibbs, senior staff scientist at the California Jet Propulsion Laboratory, builder of the Ranger and Surveyor spacecraft, saw exciting evidence here that the Moon, in its present state, may represent an evolutionary stage similar to that of a youthful Earth.

Bottom side of the Moon, never before seen from above, is revealed as starkly pitted with deep craters in this Orbiter IV telephoto taken May 11, 1967. Crater Newton, near center, is thought to be 29,000 feet deep. Here, at depths where the Sun never shines, scientists suggest explorers may find traces of water in permafrost.

35

Unusual large trough formation on the Moon's hidden side near south pole runs due north into a double crater, more than 150 miles long. Photographed by Orbiter IV, the scar is thought to be relatively young.

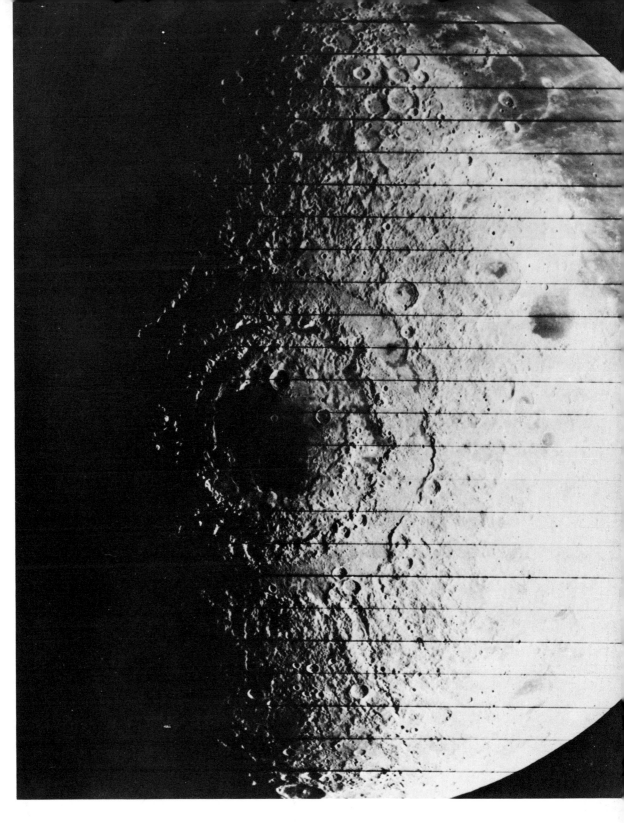

Orientale Basin, photographed from directly above by Lunar Orbiter IV, is the Moon's greatest "sore spot" where a huge meteorite slammed into it on the western rim (as visible from Earth). Impact created circular mountain ranges, some 20,000 feet high, called the Cordilleras. Oceanus Procellarum (Sea of Storms) is visible at upper right.

37

Remarkable photograph of far side of the Moon was taken by Orbiter III in 1967, revealing the mysterious black floor of crater Tsiolkovsky, first seen from the Russian spaceship Lunik III in 1959. Crater was named for Soviet "Father of Rocketery," Konstantin E. Tsiolkovsky.

THE APOLLO STORY

"In the beginning, God created the Heaven and the Earth . . ." — Christmas Eve, 1968, message from crew of Apollo 8.

MORE THAN A full year before the late President John F. Kennedy committed this nation to a manned lunar landing in 1961, Project Apollo got under way as a NASA program. On July 29, 1960, when the program was first revealed at an industry conference, the initial mission plan closely followed the direct-shot concept of Jules Verne.

Initial lunar base sites were proposed in highlands near the craters Agrippa and Aristotles, and another near the crater Kepler in the Ocean of Storms, chosen because it would be easiest to hit with a purely ballistic trajectory, an overwhelming consideration with fuel and thrust at a minimum.

Imaginative engineers like Krafft A. Ehricke, program director for the Centaur rocket, began to assemble ideas for gigantic launch vehicles. At Cape Canaveral (now Cape Kennedy) a futuristic moonport began taking shape.

The moonship itself remained a paper project until President Kennedy's

The first men to fly around the Moon. Astronauts James A. Lovell, Jr., William A. Anders and Frank Borman brought to reality Jules Verne's prediction that man would one day rocket to the Moon and back. Theirs was man's first trip to another planet.

Apollo landing sites.

challenge to industry brought the Apollo craft into being. By January, 1962, North American Aviation held the Apollo contract and the big race to the Moon was on. (Russia was already well along in space technology.)

NASA's original proposal called for a moonship to be boosted by a Saturn V rocket on a direct-ascent trajectory, to hit the Moon the way a duck shooter wings a bird by aiming ahead and letting the duck fly into the shot. Solid propellants at the time looked best—liquid fuel technology was in its infancy.

Something happened in April, 1962, to change the mission significantly. Dr. John C. Houbolt, an obscure scientist at NASA's Langley Research

Center, proposed something so radical that at first he was laughed at. His concept, called LOR (Lunar Orbit Rendezvous), was finally believed and became a part of the Apollo program. It was basically so simple others quickly claimed credit for thinking of it first. Its essence was the LM—a bug-like Lunar Module that could separate from the lunar orbiting Command Module and ferry two of the three crewmen to the Moon's surface and back.

In January, 1967, while the time was drawing near to man-rate the Apollo spacecraft, something happened to underscore the deadliness of outer space. A monster solar flare hurled earthward, the most violent interplanetary storm ever recorded. The solar shock wave came and passed, leaving scientists wondering whether Apollo astronauts could survive such giant solar winds. Then, 16 days later, tragedy struck unexpectedly when fire erupted inside the moonship during a routine ground test at Cape Kennedy. Three astronauts died in the fire—Lieutenant Colonel Virgil I. Grissom, Lieutenant Colonel Edward B. White and Lieutenant Commander Roger B. Chaffee.

Design changes corrected the fire hazard and finally, on October 11, 1968, the moonship was fully man-rated with the flight of Apollo 7, flown by astronauts Walter M. Schirra, Jr., Donn Eisele and Walter Cunningham, an 11-day mission that proved the craft ready for the 231,000 mile

Apollo 9 crew James A. McDivitt, David R. Scott and Russell L. Schweickart made the first docking test of a Lunar Module in Earth orbital flight.

Prepare to dock! Head-on view of Apollo 9 Command Module taken from Lunar Module during critical docking checkout.

trip to the Moon.

On December 21, 1968, Apollo 8 at last streaked for the Moon, carrying astronauts Frank Borman, James Lovell, Jr., and William Anders on an incredible voyage that closely followed the flight path imagined 100 years before by Jules Verne.

Four days later, on Christmas Eve, the firm voice of Air Force Captain Frank Borman spoke to all the people of planet Earth: "Apollo 8 has a message for you." There followed the emotional and thought-provoking reading of Genesis by each of the three men, so far away on their lonely flight.

"In the beginning," Major Anders' voice intoned, "God created the Heaven and the Earth . . ."

Man had reached the Moon, though there would be no landing. It was mankind's greatest technological triumph to date, one that would open the way to manned exploration of the solar system. It also gave man his first close-up look at the Moon, a sight never before seen except by remote television.

Drawing at left shows how Apollo 9 Command and Service Modules held position as LM Pilot Russell Schweickart maneuvered ascent stage to first Apollo docking. Above, Astronaut Dave Scott stands in the open hatch of Apollo 9 Command Module to photograph docked LM.

Just as Jules Verne's Moon travelers had gazed in awe as they skimmed the lunar surface, so the Apollo 8 crew studied the breathtaking scene below them. "Langrenus is quite a huge crater with a central cone . . . the walls are terraced, about six or seven terraces on the way down."

Passing over the future landing site of Apollo 11, Lovell remarked, "It certainly looks like we picked a more interesting place on the Moon to land in. It looks like a sand pile my kids have been playing in for a long time!"

The crew experienced a disturbing wobble as they whirled through the lunar orbit, slight variations produced by the gravity of massive concentrations of dense material lying below the lunar mares. Called *Mascons*, they were first discovered by unmanned Orbiters and are believed to be possibly buried asteroids.

Two more Apollo test flights were necessary before man could at last land on the Moon. Apollo 9, flown by Astronauts Jim McDivitt, Dave Scott and Russell Schweickart, completed the first manned test in space of the LM (lunar module), the first docking and the first EVA (extra-vehicular activity) in the Apollo program, during a flight of 151 Earth orbits lasting 241 hours 53 seconds.

The last preparatory flight, Apollo 10, was a final test of the LM, in a lunar orbit. Except for an actual landing, the crewmen, Tom Stafford, John Young and Eugene Cernan, accomplished a complete Moon mission in eight days.

Like the crew of Apollo 8, they described in detail more never-before-seen lunar features as they whirled around the Moon . . . a boulder field on the side of a crater that looked like a "pine forest" . . . a "volcano, all white on the outside but definitely black on top" . . . the Moon's backside, "lit up like a Christmas tree" with earthshine.

Finally, Stafford and Cernan crawled into the LM, separated from the Command Module, and twice swooped down to within 10 miles of the lunar surface for a close, hard look at the site in the Sea of Tranquillity where Apollo 11 would finally land.

"Okay, we're leaving Sidewinder," reported Cernan to Houston Control. "I've got Censorinus A . . . here. Hey, I tell you, we are low, we are close, babe! This is it and it really does looks pretty smooth down there, surprisingly enough! Censorinus A has huge boulders all around the rim of it, falling on the inside and outside. Okay, I've got Maskelyne out here on my right side. We are coming up on Boot Hill and it is very easy to distinguish . . . I see the craters that are going to lead us right into the landing site! We've got Duke Island on the left just past Boot Hill and we are coming up—I've got Wash Basin just off my right arm, very easily distinguishable . . . Ought to have Sidewinder Rille coming up on the left . . . Okay, I've got Diamondback, Diamondback Rille is very easy to see. These rilles look like they may be a couple of hunderd feet deep and very smooth . . . The best description I can give you of these rilles is of a dry desert out in New Mexico or Arizona."

The stage was set, the rehearsals completed, and the time had come for man's first visit to another celestial body. Thus it was that Neil Armstrong, Buzz Aldrin and Michael Collins made history on July 20, 1969, landing the LM of Apollo 11 exactly where Cernan and Stafford had said they would.

And when Armstrong, at the last moment, took over manual control to clear a boulder-strewn crater, he must have remembered a warning from Stafford, who reported from 9 miles above Landing Site 2: "The approach end looks a lot smoother than some of the Orbiter photos show . . . However, if you come down in the wrong area and you don't have the hover time, you are going to have to shove off!"

Armstrong did hover, and carried the day.

Apollo 10 crew Eugene A. Cernan, John W. Young and Thomas P. Stafford made final checkout of the Lunar Module in Moon orbit, did everything but land. They came to within 9 miles of the Moon's surface over Tranquillity Base.

Apollo 10 LM ("Snoopy") heads for a low pass over Tranquillity Base, leaving the Command Module to wait in orbit overhead.

48

Apollo 12 astronauts (above) are Lieut. Comdr. Alan L. Bean, Lunar Module Pilot; Comdr. Charles Conrad, Jr., Mission Commander; Comdr. Richard F. Gordon, Jr., Command Module Pilot. At right, Apollo 13 Commander James Lovell (left) and Command Module Pilot Thomas Mattingly check out the Command Module emergency exit system. Also in the spacecraft was Lunar Module Pilot Fred Haise.

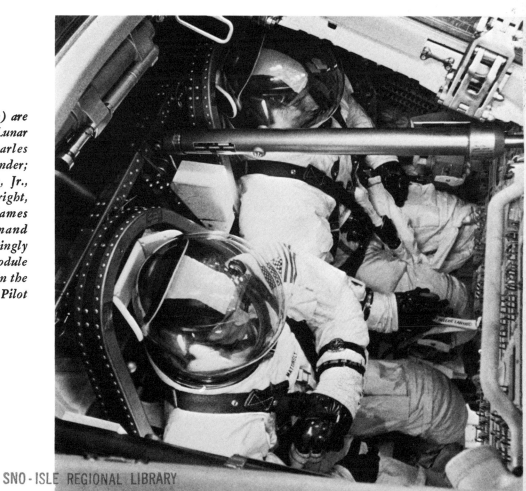

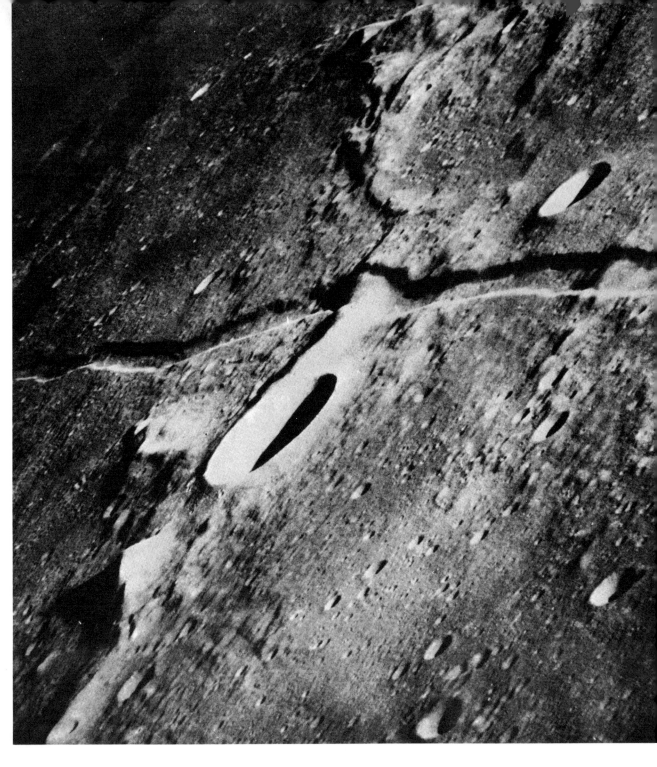

Spectacular view of "Highway U.S. 1"—a long, deep and wide rille which was seen by Apollo 10 LM astronauts as they "buzzed" Tranquillity Base for a final look before landing mission.

Exact nature of lunar rilles has long been argued by selenologists. Some believe they are ancient riverbeds, others feel they were formed by objects ejected from volcanos.

A WORLD OF GLASS, BUBBLES AND BEADS

IN THE SUMMER of 1969, scores of scientists gathered at the NASA Lunar Receiving Laboratory in Houston, anxiously awaiting the opening of two rock boxes chock full of lunar samples brought back to Earth by Apollo 11's crewmen. In the cold light of university and government laboratories, what would the contents reveal? As it turned out, they were virtual Pandora's boxes, the secrets of which would be a long time unfolding.

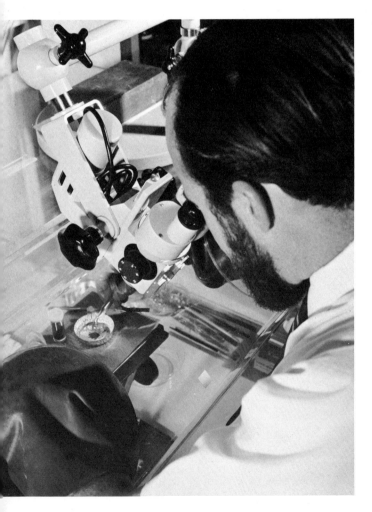

"We were not prepared for the many surprises that turned up," said Dr. Gerald J. Wasserburg, one of the Principal Investigators of the team of astrogeologists at Houston. He listed five:

1—The surface rocks were profoundly ancient—some of them 3,500,000,000 years old, comparable to the oldest exposed Earth rocks ever found (in the Minnesota River Valley).

2—The erosion rate of lunar surface rocks was much slower than anticipated — only one millimeter per million years.

3—The Moon's surface is covered with tiny glass bubbles and beads, about the size of BB shot, comprising 10 percent or more of the lunar soil.

4—Surface rocks are pitted with myriad "zap pits" and are coated with fused glass, the result of cosmic bombardment.

5—Inside the rocks appear crystalline structures of clarity and beauty, unlike the cloudy quartz of earth granite.

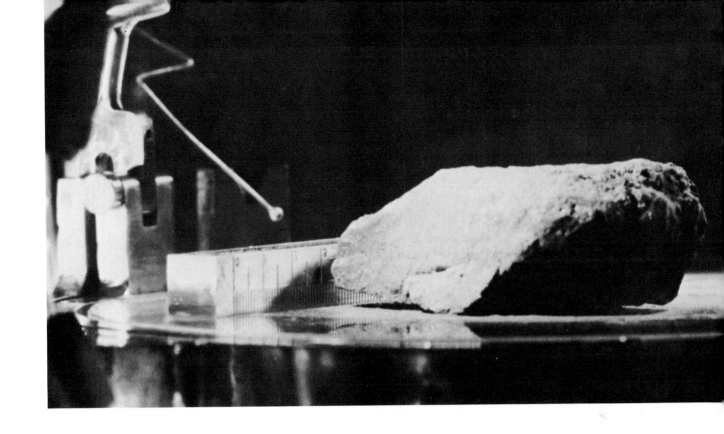

First lunar rock sample photographed in detail at Houston's Lunar Receiving Laboratory. Early look showed rock to be igneous—a granular, fine-grained rock rich in iron magnesium. Dr. Harold C. Urey, noted Moon expert, admits that rocks brought back by Apollo 11 astronauts proved to be a complete surprise. "No one anticipated what we are finding," he said. "No one has a good explanation of how [the Moon] got that way!"

The Moon rocks, found to be chemically unlike any known terrestrial rock or meteorite, literally shot down a theory that glassy, button-shaped objects called *tektites*, found scattered over the Earth, are of lunar origin. They also posed these new mysteries:

Were the glass beads formed by the impact heat of meteor strikes or by volcanic eruption?

What caused the strange cohesiveness of the brown-black lunar dust that clings like wet sand?

How did the strange "breccia" accretions form, with their clusters of amber beads and metallic particles?

Why is there an abundance of such elements as titanium, potassium, thorium and uranium on the Moon, more than ten times the amount expected to be found?

In the oldest Moon rocks, astrogeologists hope to find the key to such questions as how the Earth-Moon system was formed. Already they have determined the age of our Solar System as about 4,600,000,000 years, the same age as meteorites which reach our planet.

Thus, somewhere on the Moon they hope to find similarly aged primordial rocks, possibly in the highlands, representative of features formed in the early stages of planetary development, features long since destroyed or altered beyond recognition on Earth.

An official NASA meeting was called for January 5, 1970, in Houston, to assess what astrogeologists had learned from the 48 pounds of Apollo 11 Moon samples. Even before this scientists had been constantly under pressure to gear their laboratory study to what future Apollo crews would

Laser Ranging Retro-Reflector (LRRR) left on the Moon by Apollo 11 astronauts measured accurately Earth-Moon distance by reflecting back laser pulses 2½ miles wide and 10 feet long, like "pancakes."

From Apollo 12 on, astronauts will be carrying ALSEPs (Advanced Lunar Surface Experiments Packages) with special detectors to probe mysteries of the lunar surface and its environment.

Apollo astronauts found this crater on Moon's farside.

bring back. While scientists wanted more time between flights to analyze the lunar samples, the spaceship engineers and astronauts hoped to fly often enough to maintain a high degree of proficiency.

Although the lunar highlands offered the most challenging goal to the scientists, with the possibility of finding still older Moon rocks, the dangers of mountain landings were obvious. Hence, Apollo 12's target assignment was a relatively smooth equatorial site near crater Lansberg in the Sea of Storms, where two unmanned soft-landers, Surveyor 3 and Luna 5, had preceded them. An alternate site lay further west, a shift necessary to land on the cooler shadow terminator at dawn in the event of a time slip.

While engineers hoped that the Surveyor 3 spacecraft could be visited by Apollo 12's crew—Navy pilots Commander Charles Conrad, Jr., Lieutenant Commander Alan L. Bean and Commander Richard F. Gordon—Dr. Wasserburg in Houston saw little practical value in the visit, unless the men could "bring back a piece of its mirror" to see how many meteor-

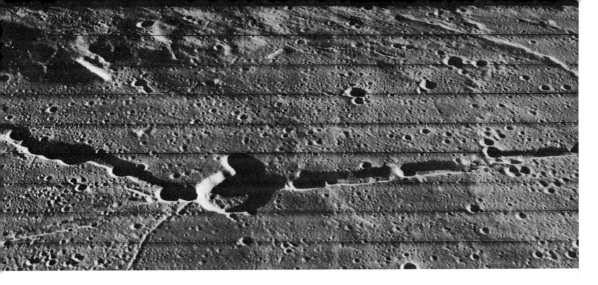

Close-up view of Hyginus crater, the "chuckhole" that appears in the middle of Hyginus Rille. Crater is 6½ miles across, 2,600 feet deep. Hyginus lies between Sinus Medii and Mare Vaporum, is being considered as a target for Apollo 19 mission.

ites had struck the craft since it bounce-landed three times on April 20, 1967. (The descent-engine didn't shut off on time. When it finally came to rest, the spacecraft squatted on the inner slope of a medium-sized crater, tilted 14 degrees.)

While no firm Apollo landing schedule had been set, future manned flights were expected to come every four months through 1972. Most attractive sites, within the limitations of mission requirements, appeared to be:

Apollo 13: A formation called Fra Mauro, on the western equatorial highlands mantled with ejecta from the Imbrium basin impact (see Chapter II). This crew may drill through the mantle to the pristine core.

Apollo 14: Censorinus, a recent small impact structure in the uplands south of where Apollo 11 landed in the Sea of Tranquillity.

Apollo 15: The Littrow Rim, a rille network north of Tranquillity Base.

Apollo 16: Tycho, the most prominent crater seen from Earth, where Surveyor 7 soft-landed in 1968.

Apollo 17: The Marius Hills, a volcanic complex on the great ridge system running down through the Ocean of Storms, resembling the volcanic piles of Mt. Rainier and Mt. Hood.

Apollo 18: Schröter's Valley, a 4,300-foot deep sinuous rille in the Aristarchus plateau, where strange ruby-red glows have indicated possibly recent volcanism.

Apollo 19: Hyginus crater and its spectacular rille.

Apollo 20: Copernicus, the most conspicuous Moon feature visible from Earth. This is a 60-mile-wide crater with towering 1500-foot-high central

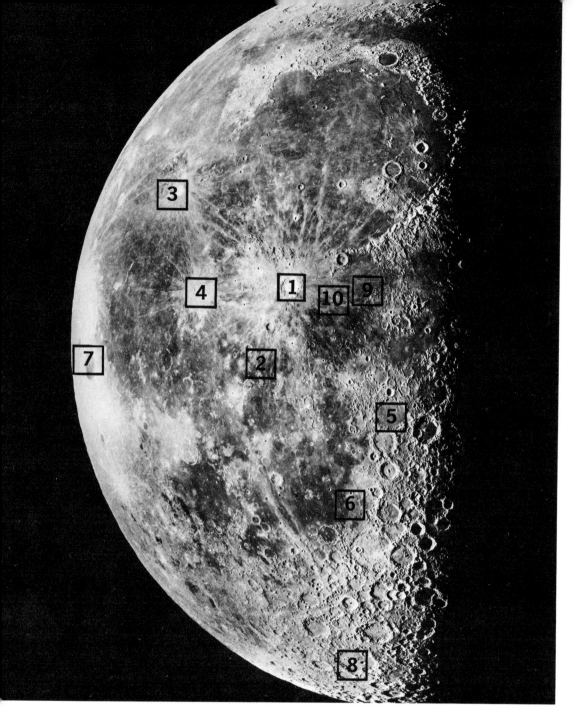

Targets of interest on west side of Moon include (1) crater Copernicus (2) Apollo 12 target site (3) Aristarchus (4) Kepler (5) Ptolemaeus (6) the Straight Wall (7) Mare Orientale (8) Clavius (9) Surveyor 4 and 6 (10) Surveyor 2.

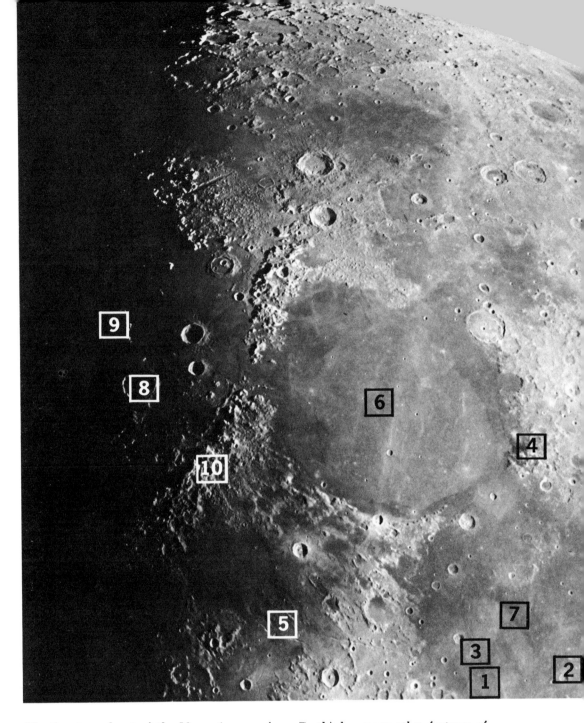

Northeast quadrant of the Moon (as seen from Earth) has many other features of interest: (1) Tranquillity Base, (2) crater Maskelyne, (3) Surveyor 5, (4) Littrow Rim, (5) Hyginus Rille, (6) Mare Serenitatis, (7) Mare Tranquillitatis, (8) Archimedes crater, (9) Mare Imbrium, (10) Apennines Mountains.

peaks, which could be explored with lunar flying vehicles following a landing inside the crater. Such central peaks are thought to have been formed by explosive rebound after meteor impacts.

On these far-ranging Apollo flights the astronauts will be carrying sophisticated ALSEPs (Advanced Lunar Surface Experiment Packages) containing active and passive seismometers, magnetometers, solar wind experiments, suprathermal ion detectors, cold cathode ion gauges, heat flow experiments and charged-particle lunar environment experiments.

Even so, according to Dr. Wasserburg, what we can learn from ALSEPs will in no way compare with what we can discover by bringing lunar material back for analysis in complex Earth laboratories.

Among Earth scientists runs an undercurrent of high competition to press for lunar experiments in which they have special interests. To quote Dr. Harold Urey, "Each person sees exactly what he expected to find there —evidence of volcanism, of movement of dust, of fragmented material, liquid water, and so forth." Early in this century, the noted Harvard astronomer, W. H. Pickering, went so far as to report seeing snow and water action on the Moon, vegetation and even small animals swarming inside the crater Eratosthenes. Today, now that we know the Moon is devoid of life, our scientific interest is more in its origins, as a means of learning more about the Earth.

"The Moon is a real fossil in the sky, and probably resembles what we will find on Mars," Dr. Wasserburg stated.

Until such time as we establish permanent Moon bases, for astronomical, seismological, magnetometrical and other long-range research, "there is no substitute for bringing Moon rocks home to study."

Even space stations now on the drawing boards will be limited in what can be achieved, according to Wasserburg. "It will be a hundred years before such space stations will become sufficiently sophisticated flying laboratories for what we hope to accomplish."

Nevertheless, the search goes on and little by little man is extending his range of lunar exploration, not only with improved landing craft, lunar rovers and lunar flyers, but with ambitious plans for complete cities on the Moon and orbiting lunar space stations able to support up to one hundred men.

Each new flight will bring back new discoveries to open whole new fields of scientific investigation, and to pose new challenges for daring space adventurers who have now begun a fantastic program for roaming on foot over the distant planets.

Crater Tycho, prominent crater where Surveyor 7 soft-landed, may be the target for Apollo 16 mission to the Moon. Black square encloses area of which a 5-by-5-foot mosaic was constructed showing surface features as small as 3 yards wide. Picture taken by Orbiter V.

Telescopic view of crater Alphonsus (the lower one) where Russian astronomer Kozyrev spotted eruption. Ranger 9 landed here, and future Apollo landing may take astronauts down for a close look at what may be a still-active volcanic region. Crater Ptolemaeus at top.

This is the 150-mile-wide crater Clavius near the Moon's south pole, which Jules Verne's astronauts described as being a volcano. Little is known of the polar regions of the Moon, where some scientists expect water will be found as permafrost.

BEYOND APOLLO

"Early upgrading of lunar exploration capability beyond the basic Apollo level, including enhanced mobility, and lunar rovers, is important to safe and efficient realization of significant returns over the longer term. An orbiting lunar station, followed by a surface-base, building upon Earth-orbital space station and space transportation system developments, could be deployed as early as the latter half of the 1970 decade. Extension of manned lunar activity beyond upgraded Apollo capability should include consideration of these options."
—*Space Task Force Report to the President, Sept., 1969.*

THEY CALL IT barnstorming the Moon, in the manner of the gypsy flyers who brought aviation to grass-roots America after World War I, in flimsy winged craft called Jennies. Now, half a century later, we are seeing a new breed of adventurers spreading out across the surface of the Moon, to fully develop the rich potential of exploring other worlds.

Our new national space goal, authorized by President Richard M. Nixon, once more places the United States in the forefront of man's restless probing of the solar system.

Just as the half-million pilots flying America's skyways today are following the lead of such pioneers as Charles A. Lindbergh, so are new teams of astronauts and space scientists preparing to follow the leadership of Commander Neil A. Armstrong and his crew of Apollo 11 in penetrating our ever-expanding horizons of space flight.

With one eye on future planetary explorations, we in this decade will develop deep-space penetration techniques closer to home, in the cislunar region between Earth and the Moon, and on the Moon itself.

One of the biggest problems of space exploration has always been its almost exorbitant cost—the first orbital flights cost up to $1,000,000 per pound of payload. By contrast, the Apollo flights atop Saturn V boosters now orbit at a cost of approximately $500 a pound, but to make space activity the commonplace utility it will eventually become, says NASA, the cost of space transport must be reduced to $50 a pound and eventually to $5 a pound.

To achieve this we will employ reusable space shuttles which will prob-

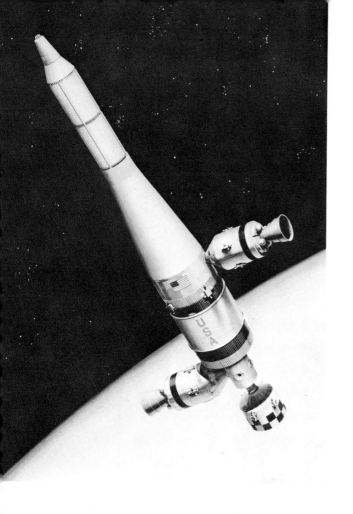

Lunar space stations now on the drawing boards may be orbiting the Moon in the late 1970's. At top left, a nuclear power plant is located at the tapered end of station, with Apollo modules attached at the other end. Upper right, proposed cylindrical space station, 33 feet in diameter, will provide shirt-sleeve environment for laboratory workers. At left, early concept of a lunar orbiting space station utilizes fanlike solar panels for power supply. Opposite page: 1980 Space Base concept proposed by NASA will be a cluster of space stations shaped like a gigantic Tinker Toy.

1980 SPACE BASE CONCEPT

ably take off from major airports with little or no noise. They will go into Earth orbit, exchange crews and cargo, and return for a horizontal landing. Such space shuttles can be in operation by 1976, said Dr. George E. Mueller, NASA's Associate Administrator for Manned Space Flight.

By utilizing existing space hardware, our first space station, with some 10,000 cubic feet of volume, can be constructed from the Saturn upper stage, launched into orbit, outfitted and used as a base for experiments, observations and other work in space. Preliminary design work on this S-IV stage already has been done by McDonnell-Douglas.

The Presidential Space Task Group has defined this space station module as the basic element of future manned activities in Earth orbit, of continued manned exploration of the Moon, and of manned expeditions to the planets. It will be a permanent structure, operating continuously to support from 6 to 12 occupants who can be replaced at regular intervals. Operating as a permanent manned space station in lunar polar orbit, it will serve as a base from which expeditions can be sent to any point on the Moon's surface.

By joining together several space station modules we can construct a complex space base, resembling nothing more than a gigantic Tinker Toy, and able to house from 50 to 100 men, said the Task Force. Here, in this man-made satellite of a satellite, will be a fantastic space laboratory wherein a broad range of physical and biological experiments will be performed.

Also envisioned for the latter part of this decade is a Space Transportation System to include three important elements:

• A reusable chemically fueled shuttle operating between Earth and a low-Earth orbit station as an airline-type vehicle.

• A chemically fueled reusable space tug, to be used as a transfer vehicle between the lunar-orbit base and the lunar surface.

• A reusable nuclear stage for transporting men, spacecraft and supplies between Earth orbit and lunar orbit. The NERVA nuclear engine development program, now under way, provides the basis for this stage and represents a major advance in propulsion capability.

Down the line are plans to fly such a modular space station under nuclear propulsion to the planet Mars, sometime in the 1980's. But until that day comes, the Moon itself will be our celestial proving ground for building distant colonies in space.

There will be many advantages to an orbiting lunar space station as a base of future exploration of the Moon, in addition to the economic benefits of a long operational life. Among the most significant will be its ability to carry either solar or nuclear power supplies of up to 100 kilowatts.

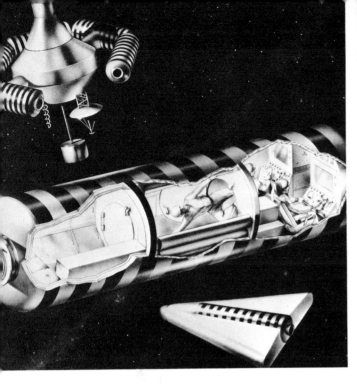

Double-walled orbiting space station could be assembled into a Space Base, from which winged shuttle vehicle would operate to Earth or Moon.

Early concept of Space Station from which trans-planetary craft could be launched to Mars or Venus on 500-day voyages.

All aboard for the Moon! Future Moonports may resemble this concept of what space travelers will enjoy by the end of this decade.

Inside orbiting space stations crews of technicians will monitor instruments in scientific laboratories where new sciences may develop.

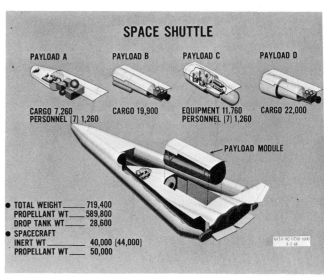

SPACE SHUTTLE

PAYLOAD A	PAYLOAD B	PAYLOAD C	PAYLOAD D

CARGO 7,260
PERSONNEL (7) 1,260

CARGO 19,900

EQUIPMENT 11,760
PERSONNEL (7) 1,260

CARGO 22,000

← PAYLOAD MODULE

- TOTAL WEIGHT_____ 719,400
  PROPELLANT WT____ 589,800
  DROP TANK WT_____ 28,600
- SPACECRAFT
  INERT WT_____ 40,000 (44,000)
  PROPELLANT WT____ 50,000

NASA HQ 17C68-0800
5-2-68

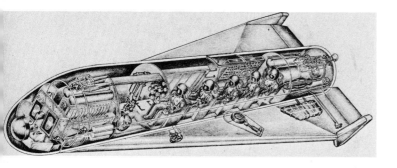

Contractors today are at work designing and building space shuttle vehicles, ferries and tugs to form a space transportation system for tomorrow. At top left is the M2-F2 lifting body research ship, already flying. It is the prototype of coming reentry vehicles that can land anywhere at will. Middle left, a space shuttle vehicle concept. Lower left is a Space Tug called the SLOMAR for remote adjustment of nuclear power systems. Above, NASA's proposal to industry for Space Shuttle.

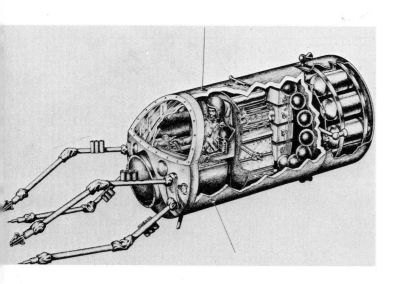

Equally important to the future of lunar explorations are chemically- or nuclear-powered space tugs in which 6-man crews will drop down from the lunar-orbiting station to any point on the Moon, to stay there from two to four weeks at a time. Back in the space station, they will accomplish scientific analysis of samples brought up, and resupply the space tug for the next down mission.

Among the advantages of orbiting space stations and lunar bases will be the installation of great stellar observatories from which to scan the distant reaches of the cosmos, to learn still more about the origins and the nature of the universe. And on the far side of the Moon, effectively shielded from Earth-generated electrical static, giant radio telescopes will be able to peer still further out.

Imagine such a telescope, able to penetrate the galactic (space) dust clouds which obscure 90 percent of the sky! Imagine being able to look back through time itself, actually seeing distant galaxies 1,000,000,000 light years away—that were there a billion years ago!

Our own galaxy, according to Dr. Gerald Wasserburg, is roughly 10,000,000,000 years old, hence we would be looking backward toward the beginnings of time itself. According to one accepted theory, all the materials in all the galaxies were once packed together in a supercondensate which in the beginning exploded, resulting in what cosmologists call the expanding universe concept. By finally determining the age of primordial Moon rocks, we may one day be able to learn when our solar system was created, and where we fit into the unsounded depths of the universal time pool.

While astrogeologists and cosmologists ponder such philosophical matters, our exploration of the Moon will be bringing into sharp focus a closer perspective of the Earth itself, an awareness that men of all nations live together on one small planet, probably the only inhabited planet in the entire solar system.

James D. Burke, head of a NASA Jet Propulsion Laboratory team studying future lunar scientific exploration techniques, put it this way: "We are strongly reminded that the Earth itself is a spaceship, that we are all here together on it and should take better care of it."

On the next pages, the shape of future space exploration during the next decade is suggested pictorially in exciting new projects which already have been seriously proposed by engineers and scientists.

Whatever man's role becomes in space, wherever his restless wanderings lead him, the next ten years can determine the path he will eventually follow, either toward ultimate peace for all mankind, or extinction.

Project Selena is a remarkable plan for utilizing huge, reusable single-stage rockets three ways—carrying passengers, carrying cargo and being converted to lunar housing facilities.

Moon bases are part of the national planning for future exploration of the lunar surface. Inside huge domed lightweight structures will be constructed whole Moon cities, with oxygen and water obtained from rocks by nuclear power. Serious scientists now question whether these would be practicable or even possible, but once people said we'd never go to the Moon!

Survival shelters for lunar explorers could be launched from Earth and soft-landed on the Moon where needed, emplaced by remotely-controlled robots in this unusual scheme.

Nuclear rockets will be used in advanced lunar exploration. Here are two concepts of what astronauts will someday be flying to visit permanent bases on the Moon.

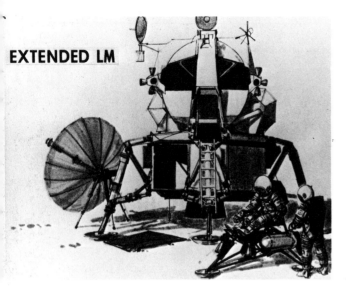

EXTENDED LM

Lunar vehicles are now planned to give astronauts an extended mobility range from their initial landing sites. Top left is an Extended Lunar Module flying rig. Top right, one- and two-man lunar flyers with rocket power. Lower left, a dual-mode lunar rover. Lower right, a mole-machine to dig Moon tunnels for housing.

DUAL-MODE LUNAR ROVING VEHICLE

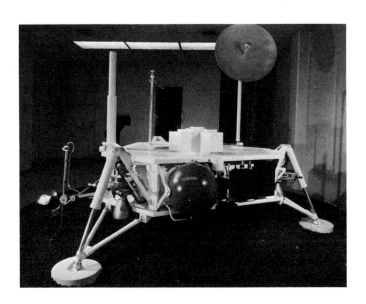

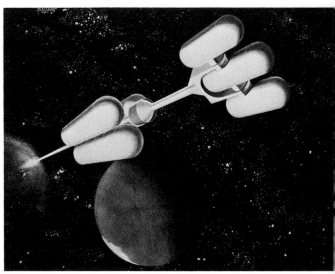

To Mars in the 1980's? This is the projected goal of the United States after we prove our capabilities on the surface of the Moon. Upper left: A Martian unmanned soft-lander, Project Viking. Upper right: a fast, nuclear-powered reconnaissance ship leaves Mars for return to Earth. Lower left: some scientists think life exists near the Martian south pole, here photographed by Mariner 7 in 1969. Lower right: A Martian outpost in the polar ice field.

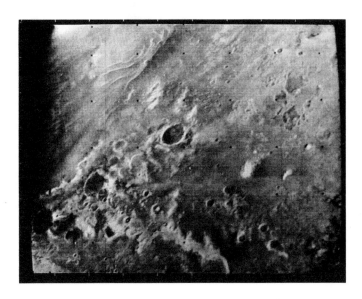

 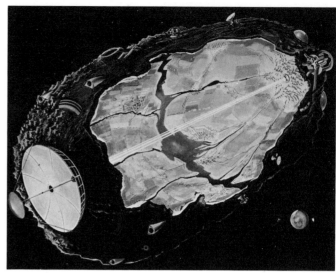

Trips to other planets of the solar system are envisioned after going to Mars. Top left: a Saturn probe. Top right: A city built within an asteroid. Lower left: Explorers depicted on the hot, cloudy planet Venus. Lower right: A mission to Jupiter, five times farther from the Sun than planet Earth.

Will we ever leave the Solar System to explore the Cosmos? Unlikely, but orbiting telescopes *already are studying the secrets of deep space, the home of wandering comets and other star clusters like the beautiful Whirlpool Galaxy, in a search for life on other worlds.*

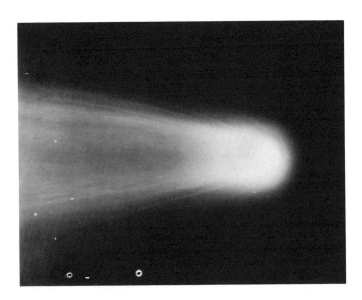

GLOSSARY

ALSEP—Advanced Lunar Surface Experiments Package.

APOGEE—Highest point in an Earth orbit.

APOLLO PROJECT—U.S. National Goal of lunar exploration by man.

APOLUNE—Highest point in a lunar orbit.

APOSELENE—See apolune.

ASTEROID—A small planet from region between Mars and Jupiter.

ASTROGEOLOGIST—A geologist concerned with study of solid matter of celestial bodies such as the Moon.

BRECCIA—A non-homogenous rocky aggregate.

CELESTIAL MECHANICS—A study of the forces that determine the orbits of celestial bodies and spacecraft.

COLUMBIA—Nickname of Apollo 11 Command/Service Module.

COSMOLOGIST—One who studies the origin, structure and space-time relationships of the universe.

CRATER—On the Moon, a bowl-shaped depression caused by a meteoric impact or volcanic action.

EAGLE—Nickname of the Apollo 11 Lunar Module that took first men to Moon's surface.

EARTHSHINE—Sunlight reflected from Earth to the Moon.

EVA—Extra-Vehicular Activity, as in "space walks."

GALAXY—One of billions of star clusters, such as our Milky Way.

IGNEOUS—Rocks formed by solidification of molten magma.

LM—Lunar module.

LOR—Lunar Orbit Rendezvous, as in docking or separation of Apollo Command/Service and Lunar Modules.

LRRR—Laser Ranging Retro-Reflector, a special "mirror" left on the Moon to measure its distance from Earth.

LASER—Light Amplification by Stimulated Emission of Radiation; a high-powered light beam.

LIFE-SUPPORT EQUIPMENT—Special environmental gear carried by astronauts on Moon, making them independent of Lunar Module while exploring.

MAGMA—Molten rock material inside Earth, Moon, etc., from which igneous rocks result by cooling.

MAGNETOMETRICAL—Pertaining to measurement of magnetic fields.

MARES—Dark lunar plains once thought to be seas.

MASCON—Massive concentrations of dense material under the lunar surface which affect orbiting spacecraft.

METEORITE—A small solid particle free-falling through space.

ORBITER—Unmanned lunar orbiting spacecraft.

PERIGEE—Lowest point in an Earth orbit.

PERILUNE—Lowest point in a lunar orbit.

PERISELENE—See perilune.

RADIO TELESCOPE—A special antenna designed to monitor non-visible radiations from deep space.

RANGER—An unmanned spacecraft project designed to photograph lunar landing sites prior to crash-landing.

RILLE—A long, narrow valley on the Moon of uncertain origin.

ROVER—A wheeled lunar vehicle, like a "dune buggy."

SEISMIC—Pertaining to earthquakes or moonquakes.

SELENOGRAPHY—Study of the Moon's physical features.

SOLAR WIND—An outpouring of radiated energy from the Sun.

SPACE BASE—An Earth- or Lunar-orbiting laboratory assembled from several space stations.

SPACE SHUTTLE—A spacecraft designed to take passengers and cargo between Earth, Moon and space bases or stations.

SPACE STATION—A single orbiting manned laboratory.

SPACE TUG—A spacecraft designed to move a space station from one orbit to another.

SURVEYOR—An unmanned lunar soft-lander spacecraft.

SYZYGY—Alignment of three or more celestial objects, such as Earth-Sun-Moon.

TECTONIC—Deformation of Earth or Moon crust that forms rocks.

TEKTITES—Button-shaped glassy objects believed of meteoric origin.

VOLCANISM—Volcanic power, as in eruption of a volcano on the Earth or Moon.

INDEX